LIBRA

23 September–23 October

PATTY GREENALL & CAT JAVOR

MQP

Published by MQ Publications Limited
12 The Ivories
6–8 Northampton Street
London N1 2HY
Tel: 020 7359 2244
Fax: 020 7359 1616
Email: mail@mqpublications.com
www.mqpublications.com

Copyright © MQ Publications Limited 2004
Text copyright © Patty Greenall & Cat Javor 2004

Illustrations: Gerry Baptist

ISBN: 1-84072-658-X

1 3 5 7 9 0 8 6 4 2

Printed in Italy

1 THE **ESSENTIAL** LIBRA

2 **RISING** SIGNS

3 **RELATION**SHIPS

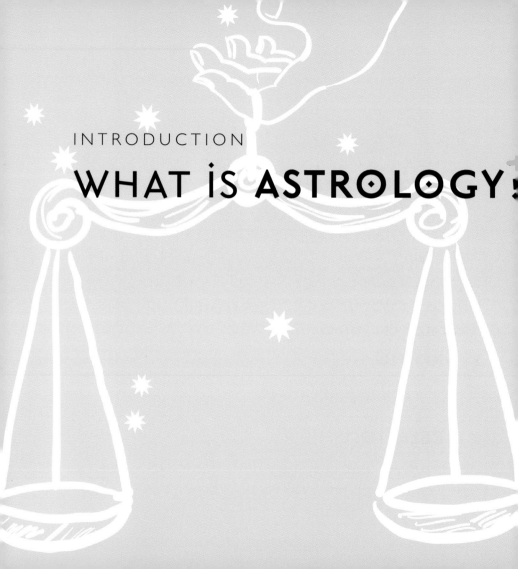

WHAT iS ASTROLOGY?

Astrology is the practice of interpreting the positions and movements of celestial bodies with regard to what they can tell us about life on Earth. In particular it is the study of the cycles of the Sun, Moon, and the planets of our solar system, and their journeys through the twelve signs of the zodiac—Aries, Taurus, Gemini, Cancer, Leo, Virgo, Libra, Scorpio, Sagittarius, Capricorn, Aquarius, and Pisces—all of which provide astrologers with a rich diversity of symbolic information and meaning.

Astrology has been labeled a science, an occult magical practice, a religion, and an art, yet it cannot be confined by any one of these descriptions. Perhaps the best way to describe it is as an evolving tradition.

Throughout the world, for as far back as history can inform us, people have been looking up at the skies and attaching stories and meanings to what they see there. Neolithic peoples in Europe built huge stone structures such as Stonehenge in southern England in order to plot the cycles of the Sun and Moon, cycles that were so important to a fledgling agricultural society. There are star-lore traditions in the ancient cultures of India, China, South America, and Africa, and among the indigenous people of Australia. The ancient Egyptians plotted the rising of the star Sirius, which marked the annual flooding of the Nile, and in ancient Babylon, astronomer-priests would perform astral divination in the service of their king and country.

Since its early beginnings, astrology has grown, changed, and diversified into a huge body of knowledge that has been added to by many learned men and women throughout history. It has continued to evolve and become richer and more informative, despite periods when it went out of favor because of religious, scientific, and political beliefs.

Offering us a deeper knowledge of ourselves, a profound insight into what motivates, inspires, and, in some cases, hinders, our ability to be truly our authentic selves, astrology equips us better to make the choices and decisions that confront us daily. It is a wonderful tool, which can be applied to daily life and our understanding of the world around us.

The horoscope—or birth chart—is the primary tool of the astrologer and the position of the Sun, Moon, Mercury, Venus, Mars, Jupiter, Saturn,

Uranus, Neptune, and Pluto at the moment a person was born are all considered when one is drawn up. Each planet has its own domain, affinities, and energetic signature, and the aspects or relationships they form to each other when plotted on the horoscope reveal a fascinating array of information. The birth, or Sun, sign is the sign of the zodiac that the Sun was passing through at the time of birth. The energetic signature of the Sun is concerned with a person's sense of uniqueness and self-esteem. To be a vital and creative individual is a fundamental need, and a person's Sun sign represents how that need most happily manifests in that person. This is one of the most important factors taken into account by astrologers. Each of the twelve Sun signs has a myriad of ways in which it can express its core meaning. The more a person learns about their individual Sun sign, the more they can express their own unique identity.

ZODIAC WHEEL

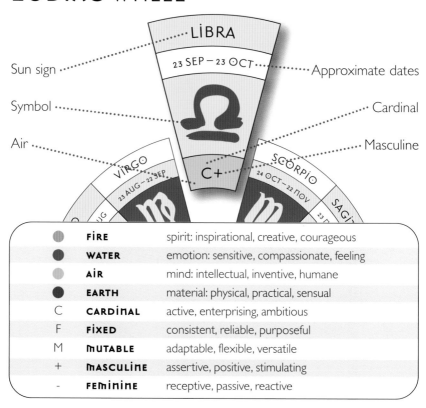

Sun sign · Approximate dates

Symbol · Cardinal

Air · Masculine

LIBRA

23 SEP – 23 OCT

VIRGO · 23 AUG – 22 SEP

SCORPIO · 24 OCT – 22 NOV

C+

●	**FIRE**		spirit: inspirational, creative, courageous
●	**WATER**		emotion: sensitive, compassionate, feeling
●	**AIR**		mind: intellectual, inventive, humane
●	**EARTH**		material: physical, practical, sensual
C	**CARDINAL**		active, enterprising, ambitious
F	**FIXED**		consistent, reliable, purposeful
M	**MUTABLE**		adaptable, flexible, versatile
+	**MASCULINE**		assertive, positive, stimulating
-	**FEMININE**		receptive, passive, reactive

ARIES
21 MAR – 20 APR

TAURUS
21 APR – 21 MAY

GEMINI
22 MAY – 21 JUN

CANCER
22 JUN – 22 JUL

LEO
23 JUL – 22 AUG

VIRGO
23 AUG – 22 SEP

LIBRA
23 SEP – 23 OCT

SCORPIO
24 OCT – 22 NOV

SAGITTARIUS
23 NOV – 22 DEC

CAPRICORN
23 DEC – 20 JAN

AQUARIUS
21 JAN – 19 FEB

PISCES
20 FEB – 20 MAR

PART ONE

THE ESSENTIAL LIBRA

RULERSHİPS

Libra is the seventh sign of the zodiac and the second Air sign. It is ruled by the planet Venus and its symbol is the Scales, which represent balance, harmony, unity, and perfect equilibrium. Libra is the only sign to be represented by an inanimate symbol; all the others are represented by humans or animals. Libra is also known as a Cardinal and Masculine sign. There are earthly correspondences of everything in life for each of the Sun signs. The part of the human body that Libra represents is the kidneys. Gemstones for Libra are coral, iolite and tanzanite. Libra also signifies windmills, sandy and gravelly fields, artists, florists, fine art, beauty parlors, boutiques, and dressing rooms in houses. It also signifies doves, strawberries, and violets.

LIBRA

The part of the human body that Libra represents is the kidneys.

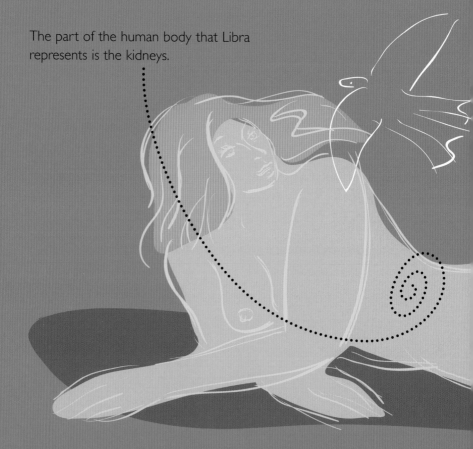

artists, fine art, violets

Florists

PERSONALITY

The grace with which Libra glides through life is both a personal virtue and a gift that Librans project out into the world. It all stems from their need to harmonize the polarities of masculine and feminine in their own inner psyche as well as the positive and negative, and aggressive and passive polarities that they encounter around them. Achieving balance and finding the perfect middle point is the basic motivation of those born under the sign of the Scales; they try to maintain complete impartiality, always seeing both sides to every story and the validity in opposing viewpoints. After all, there's a seed of rightness in every side and in everyone! Since fairness and equality are important to them they like to weigh things in the balance before passing judgment, which means that Libra is often described as an indecisive sign. However, while Librans truly understand and see all sides of a situation, generally speaking they aren't uncertain about any of it. They have an ideal of perfect harmony in their minds, which they long to find in the world, and although reality doesn't often reflect that ideal, they'll continue their search in hopeful expectation.

Part of this search means that Librans are drawn to form relationships with other people, for what they feel unable to express themselves, they look to others to express. They have an innate ability to spot the talents of others and are able to inspire those people to fulfill their potential. They will work hard to form the perfect partnership or to contribute to any joint projects that have some ideal as their goal. They also find it easy to adjust their own behavior to complement the behavior of those they meet, which makes them popular in social situations and desirable partners for romance.

Charming and genial, they love being in the company of friends and acquaintances—they are light, bright, and flirty, attracting attention like a glittering butterfly and making real connections with people thanks to their excellent mental abilities and lively conversation. Dark, heavy, brooding atmospheres bring them down; indeed, when humanity exposes its raw, crude underbelly, Libra will often walk away or turn a blind eye rather than be enveloped by disappointing reality. Their view of life is a romantic, ideal fantasy that they want to make real, so they project a pleasant, happy, and amusing image to the world, hoping that the world will reflect it back to them. They have a similar mode of operation when it comes to personal relationships: in their search for "the supreme love," they often put their partners on a pedestal, ignoring all their faults and flaws. It often comes as a shock when loved ones don't quite measure up to Libra's expectations. However, if anyone can make a relationship work, then it's a Libra. They love being in a committed, loving partnership; once they have given their heart and shared their life with another, they feel complete and this helps them to keep at bay the loneliness that otherwise would threaten to overwhelm them. Their search for mental intimacy and accord means that they're always ready to discuss the ins and outs of their relationship and are brilliant at arriving at compromises so that both partners can be happy and can keep their sense of self-esteem. However, if the relationship doesn't prove loving and doesn't offer growth or mutual support, Libra will find it difficult to sever the ties that bind. Instead, Librans may unconsciously tip the scales toward disharmony and discord so that the other person will take the initiative and end the relationship.

Ruled by Venus, and being the only sign represented by a mechanical device, Libra is considered one of the most civilized signs of the zodiac—refined and never, ever beastly! Librans are congenial, gentle, kind, and charming, and are famous for their love of beauty, good taste, and elegance. It's rare to find any Librans who are crude, rude, or rough in their physical appearance and if one was, their exterior would simply be a mask for a much more refined character that has never found the right environment to express its true self.

As an Air sign, Libra is concerned with ideas, mental images, and moral principles. Librans also have very good critical faculties. These traits combine to give them a well-tuned esthetic sense. They have a great love of beauty and of anything that is pleasing to the senses. It's as though they have a natural orientation toward anything nice! However, this has its darker side; if they are faced with people, places, or things that are unsophisticated or, worse, vulgar, then they can appear snobby, pretentious, and snooty. That's because they feel as though they couldn't possibly be expected to deal with anything uncouth, beneath them, or less than perfect. They can also sometimes come across as superficial, manipulative, and completely dependent upon others, and they do sometimes seek relationships for personal gain.

Their grace and charm, however, go a long way toward endearing them to others, and most people are willing to take the good with the bad. Librans are also peacemakers; they can be sufficiently unemotional and detached to deal rationally with contentious issues and to effect an outcome that leaves both sides feeling as if they have gained. In addition, they will add something of their own; with their smiling, uplifting, and calming presence, they are able to bring light and life to people's darkest hours.

CAREER & MONEY

Although Librans often appear to be footloose and fancy-free, they are certainly not lacking a few ambitious bones in their bodies! They like nice things, know what they want, and are not afraid to aim for the highest peak. One of their best work-related characteristics is their predisposition for being friendly, democratic, and diplomatic, and, because they need to relate to people, they often function best when they are part of a group or partnership. When they are in charge in the working environment, they have a real talent for getting the best out of people and for organizing groups and blending diverse personalities so that everyone can play their part toward achieving a collective goal. That is why they make good managers, division heads, administrators, and diplomats, and they also work fantastically well in public relations.

Their Venus-inspired, strong esthetic sense and their love of handling fine things are characteristics that make them suited to work in the world of art or in any career associated with beauty or beautiful objects. They can make the most of their natural talents as artists, composers, musicians, makeup artists, interior designers, jewelry makers, clothing designers, or designers and makers of hand-crafted furnishings. Librans also enjoy contact with other people, so they do well in careers in the retail industry, whether as buyers, senior managers, or in marketing.

But not all Librans are dynamic go-getters. Some are totally laid-back and prefer to spend as much of their time as possible enjoying life. They would be content in almost any career as long as they have minimal responsibility and the paycheck comes in so that they can spend their spare time surfing, skating, golfing, or simply sunning themselves!

Overall, however, the urge to surround themselves with lovely objects and to live in a beautiful, harmonious environment motivates them to make the money that's necessary to fulfill such desires. To earn the kind of salary that will allow them to indulge in the finer things in life—buying *objets d'art*, traveling to exotic resorts, living the high life and mixing with trendsetters— usually means that they need to be in a position of power in the workplace.

When it comes to money, Libra has the good taste never to talk about it. Librans wouldn't be caught dead comparing their salaries with someone else's; manners and etiquette simply don't allow it. However, they are clever with their cash; while they like to spend money on expensive luxuries, they'll manage to afford them because they earn a fortune, are excellent at budgeting, or are the kind of person who can spot a bargain from a mile off. They won't compromise on quality, either; it's important to them to buy things that make them feel like a million dollars.

THE LİBRA **CHİLD**

The attractive qualities of the Libra child are evident from the moment he or she comes into the world. They have a way of smiling at just the right moment and this gains them the attention they need to underpin their sense of security. They don't like to be left alone and will demand company, but so long as there is somebody close by whom they can enchant with their attempts at bubbly conversation, they will be happy little people. They possess an innate sensitivity to harmony in their environment and will respond positively to sweet, loving words and, in particular, to music, which they will play or dance to with lively enthusiasm. Librans are romantic children who will treasure most those moments when they have the undivided attention of a grown-up reading them a bedtime story about magical lands, heroic princes, and beautiful princesses. They prefer playing games in which they can act out their fantasies with others, such as "cops and robbers" or "house" and, as they get older, they enjoy board and card games. What's important for them isn't winning—although they often do win because they're usually pretty bright—but being involved in a game with someone else. The only lone activities for which they may show some inclination will be artistic things such as drawing, painting, modeling, or playing a musical instrument.

Being very sociable, they often attract a large group of friends and they like to stay in regular contact with them, so the after-school telephone bills could mount up in a Libra child's house. As Libra children grow into adolescence, maintaining their popularity is often a strong motivating force for them. This gives them the tendency to be overly agreeable and accommodating to others, which could mean that not only do they become preoccupied with relationships to the exclusion of personal achievement, but that they end up losing sight of their personal boundaries. It would be useful to remind Libra children that their natural love of beauty, harmony, and peace, along with their lively intellect is what makes them among the loveliest, most likable people to have around.

PERFECT **GİFTS**

Any gift that appeals to the senses will go down a treat with a Libra and that's a more important factor to them than the cost. However, since price is usually a reflection of quality, it wouldn't be a mistake to spend a fortune on a gift for a Libra friend if you can afford it! Although what appeals to the senses may seem like a subjective matter, it's not really. If you're buying something that appeals to the eye—a work of art, a curio, or a knickknack, for example—make sure that it's in good taste and if you're in any doubt, ask another Libra for their opinion. Librans can be particular but they'll always accept a well-considered present with a smile. It may end up in the trash when no one is looking, but they would never make the giver feel as if he or she had wasted their time or money.

Appealing to their sense of smell, sound, taste, and touch is just as important; anything rough, brash, or noisy will simply rattle their nerves. They love delicate perfumes, potpourri, and fresh flowers. They revel in classical or any beautiful music. They are partial to fine wines, expensive chocolate, caviar, and truffles. They adore silk, satin, and lace, along with tailored suits and dresses with flowing lines.

FAVORITE **FOODS**

Gastronomically speaking, Librans aren't what you'd call fussy eaters or difficult to please, but neither are they willing to eat just anything. They recognize that eating is one of life's pleasures and that, when it comes to quality, nobody should skimp. What matters most to them is the blending of the best fresh ingredients; everything should work well together to make a combination that pleases the palate. Librans would never, for example, think of serving up roast pork without apple sauce, roast lamb without mint sauce, or turkey without cranberry. As everyone knows, there are certain flavors that work beautifully together—and no one knows that better than Librans. They also have particularly refined tastebuds and are immediately aware when a dish has been under- or over-seasoned, or when the flavors are in conflict. It would be unusual for them to have a favorite meal; when they eat out with friends they're usually content to go along with what others choose, but they'll be very unhappy if some crucial flavor is missing or if the appropriate condiments aren't available. Atmosphere and etiquette are also extremely important to Librans; they like their food attractively laid out, their wine elegantly served, lighted candles on the table, music playing gently in the background, and they will always wait for everyone else to be served before they start. Food and the experience of eating with friends is important to them; it's something to be shared and enjoyed.

FASHION & **STYLE**

Whether male or female, Librans are usually beautifully attired when they step out of the door; their appearance and the effect it has on others is key to them. They aren't into making a big impact, but it has to be the right one. Elegance and exquisite taste, knowing exactly what suits them and is pleasing for others to look at—all these combine in Librans in such a way as to attract flattery and imitation. Even when they're wearing clothes that are ten years out of date, they somehow still manage to look fashionable, and when they're mooching about at home wearing their comfy old clothes, they still have a distinctly nonchalant style. Fashion is one of their pleasures; it's as interesting to them as any of the other arts and they're usually very well-informed about what's in and what's out, and which designers are hot and which are not. They can spot a designer label at a hundred paces and have no problems spending their money on beautiful, expensive, and well-made outfits, particularly if they are recognizable as designer clothes.

Floral patterns and pastel blues, greens, pinks, and yellows are not for everyone but they look lovely on Librans and even if they're wearing dark, heavy, serviceable clothes, they will usually add some softening, romantic touch to tone down an otherwise severe ensemble.

IDEAL HOMES

Whether it's a room with a view or an enchantingly beautiful garden, you can be sure that the Libra home will have something special and heavenly about it. It will have some feature that defines it and transforms it from an ordinary abode into a residence of distinction—and that means more than just a fresh lick of paint. Librans prefer to decorate their homes often enough to prevent them from becoming worn and tired-looking.

Librans' refined tastes are most apparent in their homes, for this is where they can mingle with their guests and be admired for their exquisite taste in interior design. Men and women alike enjoy a soft yet sleek quality to their home and they like to make it a place to relax in, with beautiful scents wafting through the air. When it comes to furnishings, they like traditional floral patterns but will also be happy to choose the latest interior-design trends. They tend not to hoard but like their homes to be clean and clutter-free since too much stuff creates stress. So what do they do with their possessions? Everything will either be neatly organized in cupboards or given to a charity. The Libra home is a place to be seen but not necessarily heard. Calm and quiet prevail but you might be invited for a gentle chat, a beautifully rehearsed performance on a musical instrument, or to hear a sweet song being sung.

PART TWO

Rising Signs

WHAT IS A **Rising Sign**?

Your rising sign is the zodiacal sign that could be seen rising on the eastern horizon at the time and place of your birth. Each sign takes about two and a half hours to rise — approximately one degree every four minutes. Because it is so fast moving, the rising sign represents a very personal part of the horoscope, so even if two people were born on the same day and year, and in the same place as one another, their different rising signs will make them very different people.

It is easier to understand the rising sign when the entire birth chart is seen as a circular map of the heavens. Imagine the rising sign — or ascendant — at the eastern point of the circle. Opposite is where the Sun sets — the descendant. The top of the chart is the part of the sky that is above, where the Sun reaches at midday, and the bottom of the chart is below, where the Sun would be at midnight. These four points divide the circle, or birth chart, into four. Those quadrants are then each divided into three, making a total of twelve, which are known as houses, and each of which represents a certain aspect of life. Your rising sign corresponds to the first house and establishes which sign of the zodiac occupied each of the other eleven houses when you were born.

All of which makes people astrologically different from one another; not all Librans are alike! The rising sign generally indicates what a person looks like. For instance, people with Leo, the sign of kings, rising, probably walk with a noble air and find that people often treat them like royalty. Those that have Pisces rising frequently have soft and sensitive looks and they might find that people are forever pouring their hearts out to them.

The rising sign is a very important part of the entire birth chart and should be considered in combination with the Sun sign and all the other planets!

THE RISING SIGNS FOR LIBRA (B-Cancer)

To work out your rising sign, you need to know your exact time of birth—if hospital records aren't available, try asking your family and friends. Now turn to the charts on pages 40–45. There are three charts, covering New York, Sydney, and London, all set to Greenwich Mean Time. Choose the correct chart for your place of birth and, if necessary, add or subtract the number of hours difference from GMT (for example, Sydney is approximately ten hours ahead, so you need to subtract ten hours from your time of birth). Then use a ruler to carefully find the point where your GMT time of birth meets your date of birth—this point indicates your rising sign.

Libra with **Aries** Rising

Alluring yet assertive, sweet but straight and to the point, Librans with Aries rising can be both contrary and amenable at the same time. They are the masters of gauging where other people are coming from and they are able to fit in when they have to, and yet they also manage never to lose sight of the fact that what they really want is for everyone to be in agreement. They can push and pull, give and take, or come and go, depending on what the situation requires, but this sometimes means that they have trouble satisfying their own needs. Ask these Librans what their needs are and they'll only answer "the same as everyone else's." What they must really find out is what their personal needs are without measuring them against anyone else's or against the demands of the circumstances they are in. If they know of something they want, then there's absolutely no problem; they'll instinctively go after it. These Librans usually get exactly what they are striving for, since they are very clever and ambitious people who often make a great success of life. They're energetic and inspiring and they have no difficulty in getting others to go along with their plans, but while they spend their time earnestly providing for others, their own needs frequently get ignored. They often make an enthusiastic and forthright attempt to get to know people and form alliances, because they feel happiest when in the company of anybody they can chat to and bounce ideas off.

LIBRA WITH **TAURUS** RISING

♉ Venus is the planetary ruler of both Taurus and Libra, which gives this individual a double dose of Venusian delightfulness. Libra with Taurus rising is as sweet as they come—but does tend to have at least one sweet tooth. While they put a lot of thought into their diet, exercise, fitness, and general well-being, it's difficult for them to steer clear of the sugar. These Librans are hard-working, sensible, calm, and stable. They earn enough to pay their own way, to get what they want, and to attract the good things in life. They are also very artistic and could easily write their own version of the song, "My Favorite Things." A strong thread of perfectionism runs through their veins, which means that they put a great deal of effort into maintaining their pleasing physique, wearing the right clothes, having impeccable manners, and living in a stunning home. Nobody will ever see them with a hair out of place or be able to criticize their excellent taste. Beauty is both an ideal and a necessity and anything that disrupts their esthetic sense in any way will be removed and placed out of sight. What's extraordinary is that they are able to maintain this level of beauty without sacrificing comfort, for they are loving people who adore snuggling up on a sofa and sharing genial conversation with their nearest and dearest. They will also expend a lot of time and mental energy on finding solutions to the problems of others and do their best to soothe and comfort frazzled nerves.

LIBRA WITH **GEMINI** RISING

These Librans love to discuss their creative ideas with other people, especially in cafés, bars, and other relaxed places. This is where they give birth to their plans—some work project, a plan for throwing a party, or a grand plan for life itself—then they go off and bring those plans to fruition. They can, of course, do everything on their own but the feedback and interaction that they get from others is what seems to inspire them to reach farther and to keep going. These are very productive people who are capable of taking a simple idea and developing it into something big. Highly romantic, these Librans love to love and they love the state of being in love, which, of course, is not always a state that can last forever. Idealistic in every way, they are so much fun to be around and so wonderfully spontaneous, that an outing with them could end up just about anywhere. Life for them is an intellectual game, and one that they are well-equipped to win. Their optimistic attitude and willingness to take risks mean that, even when things aren't going so well, they are able to stay positive, think around corners, and turn things to their advantage. Because there's a touch of the thrill-seeker about Librans with Gemini rising, they often find it difficult to stay in one place for long, but wherever they go and whatever they do, it will always be with style.

LIBRA WITH **CANCER** RISING

♋ They might have their gripes and complaints about their family, but the moment anyone else says anything critical about them, these fiercely protective Librans will let them know to back off. Of course, they'll let them know with a smile, since Librans wouldn't be caught dead with a look of disdain on their faces, but there'll be no doubting their intention. This is not just about family, though; Librans with Cancer rising will be the first to stand up for their loved ones or even for someone they don't know if they feel that person is being treated like an underdog. Quick as a flash, they can change from friendly to feisty—and back again once they've put their point across. Their home is often a place of comfort and beauty, somewhere welcoming and nurturing where they're always available to talk problems through with friends and family. The result is that their home is frequently full of guests. Home is also this Libra's retreat from the outside world, for although the world excites their senses, it can also impose upon them. While they need and enjoy a busy social life, they prefer to enjoy it either in the tranquil and esthetically pleasing atmosphere of their own home or at their favorite haunts.

LIBRA WITH **LEO** RISING

♌ Generous, loving, and magnanimous, these Librans are true diplomats. They are eloquent, elegant, and totally engaging, especially when they're talking about themselves—and then there's just so much to say! When they're in conversation with others, they give them their undivided attention. With Librans with Leo rising there will, of course, be a lot of talking because it's through verbal communication that they find the connection they long for and can impress people with their understanding and breadth of knowledge. They are commanding, courageous, and very likable individuals, and they possess an air of nobility that makes them walk tall and proud. There might also be a touch of the fashion-victim about them since making an impact and showing off their excellent taste is one way of attracting attention to their finer qualities, of which they are rightfully proud. With Leo rising, Libra's usual indecision is minimal; in fact, these Librans can be positively willful, which can sometimes work for them and sometimes against them. They can also be rather forceful in the way that they impose their opinions; after all, they will have spent more time than most in forming them, so they feel justified. But underneath it all, they are Librans, so they will know just when to give and they'll always do so with kind consideration.

LiBRA WiTH **ViRGO** RiSiNG

Fastidious and fussy, this Libra tries hard to please, but doesn't always go about it in a way that others find agreeable. Librans with Virgo rising tend to worry and have a habit of projecting those worries onto other people, but they are easy to soothe and then they become the kind, peaceful Librans that everyone loves. They can be exacting and if there's one thing in particular that they're exacting about, it's money. They pay attention to how much money they've got coming in and going out, almost to the point of identifying themselves through material things. They might not be the last of the big spenders, but they have a touch of the shopaholic about them since owning and accumulating desirable objects is a pleasure that they find difficult to resist. If they can learn to channel their talents into creative projects, then they are often rather successful. But it's their understanding and knowledge of other people that's their real talent and when they are working in cooperation with others, they frequently make the most stunning contributions, earning them the praise and respect they deserve. These are very clever people and if they take up the opportunities that life offers them, then they'll be able to make the best use of their considerable brainpower.

LiBRA WiTH **LiBRA** RisinG

Music seems to be in the air for Librans with Libra rising. Wherever they go, people flock to them like songbirds and if any bird needs to be coaxed from a tree, then this is the person for the job. They are the ultimate figures of grace and beauty, and even if they trip themselves up, which is incredibly rare, they will do so in time to the music, as though it were meant to happen. They look good, sound good and, because they have exquisite taste in perfume, they smell good, too. They exert a gentle command over other people and so make superb hosts, diplomats, or delegates. Kind and considerate, their smiling faces are an inspiration to those who think that you can only get what you want by being bolshie. For them, life is an open invitation to have fun and enjoy the finer things life offers and, as they optimistically engage with the world, they exude a light yet clear energy. They'll avoid arguments and disagreements, but not at any cost, for they won't put up with being pushed around. If someone wants to rain on their parade, they'll simply switch over to the sunny side of the street.

LIBRA WITH **SCORPIO** RISING

♏ You can never be sure that you know what's on the mind of Librans with Scorpio rising. For example, they may invite themselves over to a friend's place for a pleasant chat while what they really want is to flirt with their friend's roommate. So why don't they just come out and say what they're after? The reason is because it's not in their nature; it would be too revealing and too impolite, and it might hurt their friend's feelings. What is palpable about these people is their brooding sex appeal, and with their gorgeous smiles and winning ways, they're very hard to resist, especially when they're playing hard to get. But it's difficult to tell whether they are aware of their own allure; they seem so adept at tying other people's emotions up in knots yet they aren't usually doing it consciously. These are the most idealistic and romantic Librans; they long to lose themselves in a beautiful, perfect partnership and are so willing to give of themselves that they're often hurt and taken advantage of. What they need to learn to do is to spend some time testing the water before diving into a full commitment.

LIBRA WITH **SAGITTARIUS** RISING

Love and laughter are the main themes for Librans with Sagittarius rising. These Librans are distinctively optimistic, fun-loving people who seem to attract good fortune like a magnet, but that's because of their perspective on life, which is always orientated toward the light. They expect to be winners and they have an ability to throw off loss and disappointment as readily as they take out the trash. Librans with Sagittarius rising are never the sort of people to dwell on the negative aspects of life—instead, they spend much of their time having a ball, but in poised Libra style, of course, while those around them get wound up into a frenzy of amusement. And there will be plenty of people around them because being part of a group or part of society is the perfect way for them to exercise their enormous talents. They want to be involved with others on all levels—though mostly intellectual—and they put a whole heap of energy into improving the lot of those around them. They seem incredibly adept at getting others on their side and in promoting joint efforts that will make the world a better place. With a Libra with Sagittarius rising as the head of NATO or the United Nations, the planet is almost sure to be a more cooperative, joyful, and fun place to live.

LiBRA WiTH **CAPRiCORN** RiSiNG

Even when they're very young it's obvious that Librans with Capricorn rising are highly determined and ambitious individuals. They will pursue their goals with focus, persistence, and patience and, as a result, they quietly overcome each challenge, big or small. They tend to be high achievers, but not the kind who elbow everyone else out of their way as they get to the top; instead, they find their path gracefully and diligently, and with seemingly little effort or help from others. Although they appear to have a serious outlook on life, they can laugh and know how to have a good time, sometimes even laughing at themselves in an ironic manner. These particular Librans project a somewhat traditional, classic taste; they are always beautifully attired and they appreciate the sort of quality and style that never go out of fashion. They often seem wise beyond their years and have respect for polite, old-fashioned manners, which they always employ when dealing with others. They may not make their biggest impact until later in life when they have the independent means and glittering financial success that are the hallmarks of this combination, but even then they won't sit back and rest on their laurels. Action is its own reward; they know that they can always climb higher.

LiBRA WiTH **AQUARiUS** RiSiɲG

This combination makes the ultimate social butterfly; Librans with Aquarius rising eat, sleep, work, and play best when they're with other people. Even though they're unique, strong individuals with a solid character, their problem can be one of keeping a sense of their own separateness. Librans with Aquarius rising are usually well-liked and very friendly, and it would surprise them to know that they can appear aloof, cool, and detached, particularly since the truth is that they get involved—really involved—with people from all walks of life and on many different levels. Although they seem to have an inexhaustible supply of energy to power their social whirl, even they need some time to reflect, to be on their own, and to explore their creativity. However, they can't be left to spend too much time alone because they feel loneliness more than others and this can destroy their self-esteem, hence their constant compulsion to be with others. Sometimes, because these Librans with Aquarius rising can spend hours in philosophical thought and have consciously developed humanitarian aims in life, they often want to be with others simply in order to help them or to interact with them; they truly feel the need to make the world a better, happier place. Their smiling presence is often exactly what it takes to do just that.

LiBRA WiTH **PiSCES** RiSiNG

When they are young, Librans with Pisces rising are sweet, innocent, agreeable, loving characters. They often view the world through rose-tinted glasses, seeing only what is beautiful and ignoring anything unpleasant or disagreeable. Later on, things don't really change except that it gradually dawns on them that they can no longer turn a blind eye to the realities of life. They also learn to draw clearer boundaries between themselves and others, finding it easier to spell out their likes and dislikes, firstly to themselves and, eventually, to others. At times, the real world can seem a harsh place for such a delicate being, yet as they grow, they learn that life is a series of endings and new beginnings and, while retaining their soft exterior, they become strong as steel on the inside. These Librans with Pisces rising have an uncanny talent for perceiving the truth that lies deep in people's hearts and minds and are able to bring out the best—and sometimes the worst—in them. They are very interested in other people and their shy, pleasant, and often mysterious manner seems to gently offer up an open invitation for others to reveal their secrets. If they ever decide to use their creativity and their ability to tap into people's desires and dreams, for instance in some commercial partnership, then it won't be long before any project they undertake is a burgeoning success.

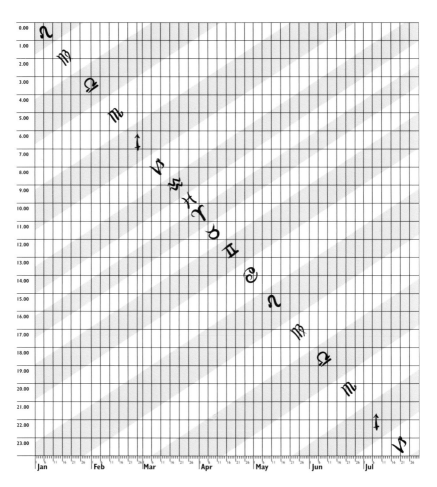

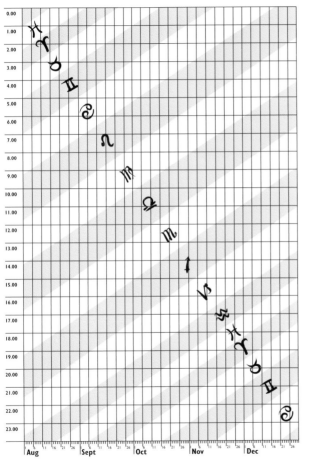

New York

latitude 39N00
meridian 75W00

♈	aries	♎	libra
♉	taurus	♏	scorpio
♊	gemini	♐	sagittarius
♋	cancer	♑	capricorn
♌	leo	♒	aquarius
♍	virgo	♓	pisces

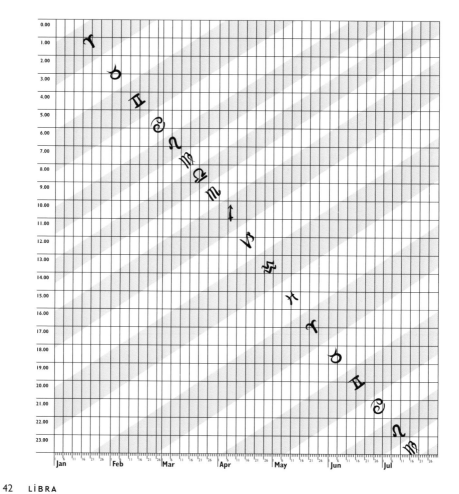

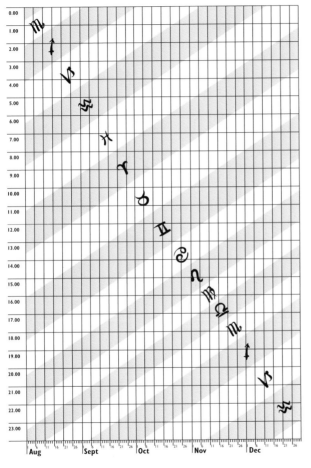

RiSiNG SiGN
CHART

Sydney
latitude 34S00
meridian 150E00

♈ aries	♎ libra
♉ taurus	♏ scorpio
♊ gemini	♐ sagittarius
♋ cancer	♑ capricorn
♌ leo	♒ aquarius
♍ virgo	♓ pisces

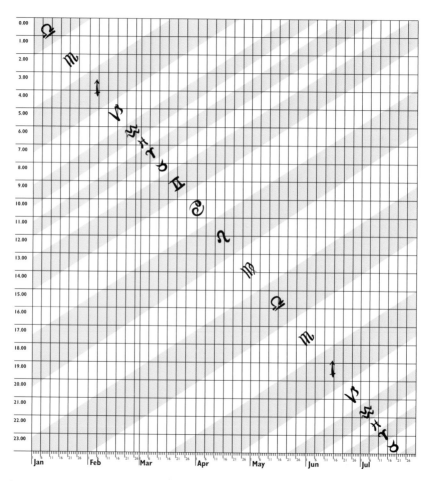

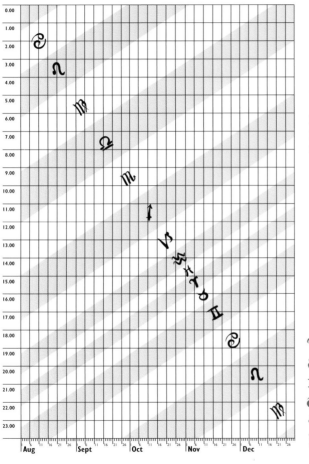

RiSiNG SiGN
CHART

London
latitude 51N30
meridian 0W00

♈	aries	♎	libra
♉	taurus	♏	scorpio
♊	gemini	♐	sagittarius
♋	cancer	♑	capricorn
♌	leo	♒	aquarius
♍	virgo	♓	pisces

PART THREE

RELATIONSHIPS

THE LIBRA **FRIEND**

Sociable, chatty, personable Librans like having friends, so much so that they often go out of their way to make the time they spend with others as pleasurable and interesting as possible. But because they can be so kind, accommodating, and brimming with stimulating conversation, people often end up outstaying their welcome and Librans are too polite to ever give the slightest indication that they'd like to show them the door. Of course, things don't always turn out like that; Librans are highly intelligent people who really enjoy getting into lofty discussions and friendly debates on almost any topic. Learning how others think helps them to understand themselves, so sitting up late into the night chatting with a friend is one pleasure that they very rarely forgo. Libra friends will always offer support to pals who are down on their luck or embarking on an exciting new venture, and they are often brimming full of excellent ideas and constructive advice, which they give freely and with love. However, if a friend ever metes out any unkind, unpleasant, or harsh treatment, then Librans will feel so low that they see no alternative but to tip the scales of hurt in the opposite direction. They'll withdraw their friendship and support. From that moment, the ball will be in the friend's court but that friend had better move fast to repair the rift. It's not like Librans to bear a grudge, but they won't easily forget the pain of insult, either.

LIBRA WITH **ARIES**

As opposite signs of the zodiac, these two are definitely attracted to one another, but their friendship may be difficult to define because they both like to push against the boundaries. They could get so drawn into each other's company that they end up excluding all other people, including other potential intimates. They have a natural ability to get each other into an excited, exuberant, wound-up state because they're both so restless. But they'll complement each other well in most situations, particularly when playing "good cop/bad cop." The phrase "bosom buddies" springs to mind with Aries and Libra.

LIBRA WITH **TAURUS**

Since both are ruled by the planet Venus, these two form the original mutual admiration society. They share a love of all things beautiful. Having said that, Libra enjoys the conceptual idea of beauty while Taurus needs to experience it in a concrete manner. When Taurus gets angry and sees a red flag waving, or gets too rigid and opinionated, Libra will have to rely heavily on the sign's diplomatic skills. In turn, it can be difficult for Taurus, who likes to stick to a definite plan, to pin down and put up with the indecisive Libra. All in all, though, these two appreciate each other and couldn't want for a friend with more interests in common.

LIBRA WITH GEMINI

Having fun comes easily to these two. They're like a couple of birds on the wing, swooping and diving around each other in playful flights of fancy. There'll be a plenty of laughter, too, since nobody appreciates the creative turn of phrase in a Gemini joke quite as much as a Libra, and when it comes to expanding the mind, Geminis know that they have found a soul mate in their Libra buddy. When they meet up together it's to have a good chat, so they'll probably spend hours in some favorite lunch spot, ordering endless steaming cups of coffee and solving the problems of the world while giggling at its absurdity.

LIBRA WITH CANCER

Although they won't disagree much, Libra and Cancer have essentially different natures. Libra likes to go to new places, meet new people, party the night away, and enjoy some flirty fun, while Cancerians prefer to party at their old, regular haunts with their familiar circle of pals. Both are very persuasive and like to have their own way, but neither is deliberately stubborn. They could make great friends, but it will just take a while for them to learn to adapt to each other's preferences. But there's enough mutual intrigue for them to combine their interests and build on for the longer term. Perhaps they'll start the party somewhere new then bring it home.

LiBRA WiTH **LEO**

♌ There's a natural sense of friendship and shared ideals between these two. Both enjoy the finer things in life and positive, uplifting vibes constantly bounce back and forth between them. Libra's charm and diplomatic skills are the perfect complement to Leo's playfulness and magnanimity. Both encourage each other to show themselves in their very best light, and when they're out on the town together, they attract admirers like moths to a flame. They make a great team socially and the only other people to get close are those who push their way in.

LiBRA WiTH **ViRGO**

♍ There are certain sensibilities that these two share that makes them natural friends. Virgo's need for order and Libra's need for harmony somehow dovetail to ensure an easy flow of thoughts and deeds between them. These two could happily spend hours together sitting over lunch and picking apart all sorts of ideas, or meeting up regularly to go to dance, yoga, or meditation classes. They don't need to go home together to experience the other's individual quirks and idiosyncrasies; they're more than happy developing an easygoing friendship based on a weekly get-together.

LIBRA WITH **LIBRA**

These two will be so congenial toward each other that they will constantly be saying, "After you," "No, no. After you." Then, "I insist. You first." Then, "Please, I don't mind. You go first." If they ever get past these excruciatingly polite exchanges, they'll realize how much time they've wasted and how they've missed out on the good stuff, which in their case consists of relating to each other on a fabulously exciting intellectual level. They also make great social pals. When the two of them mingle with others at a party, they'll flit and flirt, making everyone feel a little bit better about themselves. It's as if they were sprinkling everyone with fairy dust.

LIBRA WITH **SCORPIO**

If there were ever two friends who could share some secret verbal exchange to the exclusion of all others, then it's Libra and Scorpio. In a room full of people, you'll find these two sitting in a corner, chatting away, and exploring a whole host of intensely intellectual ideas. They'll be so totally absorbed in picking the other's point of view apart that they won't even notice that there might be a whole herd of other people who would love to join in their conversation. This pair make great friends but they'll need to do their best to include others, or else they'll be accused of cliquishness.

LiBRA WiTH **SAGiTTARiUS**

The wide-ranging philosophical bent of their Sagittarius friend is an exciting enigma to Librans who occasionally need lessons in detachment in order to fly free with their ideas. Librans, meanwhile, are perfect playmates and they make ideal, encouraging companions for Sagittarians, who long to relate to them on an intellectual level. Not only that, but they'll both love going out together, getting some fresh air, and being active. They'll make great friends and they'll also find that they offer the other enough of a challenge to stretch their minds.

LiBRA WiTH **CAPRiCORN**

This is an energetic friendship that is constantly searching for an experience of intense connection, not only between themselves, but between them and the world that they encounter through their socializing. There can be an element of healthy competition, which helps both of them to reach farther and wider in their careers. But their friendship isn't always so serious; they're always up for a party and sharing a thrilling experience helps to bring these two together. Afterward, during the post-mortem analysis that they always indulge in, is when they find their sense of accord.

LiBRA WiTH **AQUARiUS**

This friendship is both exclusively fulfilling and widely exciting because both Libra and Aquarius are able to switch between light, frivolous banter and stratospheric intellectual idealism in the blink of an eye. They are on the same wavelength so when they head out on the town together, they make a scintillating double act that others are happy to be entertained by. But even though these two get on like a house on fire, they won't faze people who might not be up to speed with their verbal exchanges. Anyone is welcome to join their gang.

LiBRA WiTH **PiSCES**

In certain situations, for instance where the champagne flows freely, these two will delight in each other's company and will find many things to talk about and empathize with. At other, more sober moments, though, while they'll respect each other's position, the conversation could go a little flat. Pisces likes to go off on a tangent, exploring the surreal aspects of life and sometimes diving into its depths, particularly when it comes to emotional issues, while Libra prefers to skim the surface, remaining light-hearted and being careful to avoid those uncomfortable dark corners of human consciousness.

THE LiBRA WOMAN iN LOVE

She's fun, she's flirty, she's flighty, but she's fantastic! Having been born under a sign that's ruled by amorous Venus, love and relationships are extremely important to this lady. Her basic aim in love is to be able to merge with another and make a perfect whole. But although that may be her aim, Lady Libra's no pushover. In fact, she's far from being one. A man either fits her criteria or he doesn't and, depending on which it is, he'll either stay or he'll have to go. She needs to get along with people in such a way that the relationship is in everyone's best interests. She understands the importance of looking at things from the other person's point of view and of reaching a compromise so that harmony can be restored. Arguments and fits of temper are things that the Libra lady simply doesn't do and neither will she put up with that kind of behavior from her partner. No matter how passionately she may fall in love, tempestuous displays of emotion, like throwing plates across the room or shouting and slamming doors, don't form part of her way of operating. For her, it's peace and love, or it's nothing.

Any potential partner should know that Lady Libra responds with love to romantic demonstrations of feeling through art, poetry, and music. She's refined in her taste and looks for that refinement to be reflected in her partner. She wants her man to embody her need for beauty and good taste, so she'll never tolerate bad language or questionable hygiene. She also appreciates plenty of verbal communication from her mate and appreciation of her lovely, artfully planned appearance—after all, she usually goes to great lengths to look as good as she does. The more time she can spend talking to her partner and learning about him on an intellectual level, the closer and more secure she'll feel. But that's not to suggest that her idea of love is only in her head. Far from it. She's a highly romantic, sensuous being; she just happens to prefer to get things straight in her mind first rather than simply follow her feelings.

Lady Libra is a woman who indulges in the pleasures of life. She loves good food and wine, fine clothes, and jewelry. Given a choice for a weekend getaway between camping and flying off to Paris in five-star style, there'd be no competition; she'll prefer Paris every time. After all, the stores on a campsite simply don't compare to European haute couture, and who would bring her the hot towels she needs to wipe her mouth and fingers after a meal in the middle of a field? Partners beware; her love of pleasure sometimes borders on extravagance.

When she's single, the Libra lady is a very social, flirtatious woman who's deeply attracted to the pursuit of love. She enjoys trying out a variety of bedroom playmates, but once she's committed herself to a relationship, that commitment is so powerful that it's very unlikely she'd ever be unfaithful—unless of course, her partner were to make her desperately unhappy.

LiBRA WOMAN WiTH **ARiES MAN**

 In love: The Aries man and the Libra lady will be attracted to each other from the first time their eyes meet across that proverbial crowded room. This fiery man will be just wild about her overtly feminine, captivating charm, and it will inspire him to show her his own special brand of charisma. She'll be completely unable to stop herself from responding to his energetic pursuit with come-hither looks. They are both social creatures, but even when they find themselves at the most exciting of parties, they'll be leading each other in a dance of prey and predator, rather than joining in the party. Who captured who first? Now, that is the question! Each would like to think that it was he who did all the chasing. After all, an Aries man is very proud of his ability to get exactly what he goes after. But the Libra lady has the seductive techniques of a siren, and she knows it, even if she does like to play coy. Once committed, the Aries man and Libra woman have a natural ability to get each other going when the going gets tough. They'll complement each other perfectly in most situations. However, they may have very different ideas of what is best for each within the relationship. Aries can be very defiant and can upset the Libra lady's need for harmony. As long as that initial spark of attraction stays alive, and both have the energy to keep it fanned, this union will last long after all others have fallen by the wayside.

In bed: When the Aries man pushes his way into the Libra woman's bedroom, he'll find scented sheets, soft lights, and romantic music. Was this all planned? Had she laid a trap and made him think that it was all his idea to walk into it? Who cares? He'll love it. Plus, he has a fire in him that will tangle those sheets, outshine the lights, and make her feel like she's sweating at a rock concert! On her side, the Libra lady is quite talkative in the bedroom and understands the stunning effect of using sexily spoken words to encourage and excite her Aries lover. This fires up his passion even more, making him capable of eliciting countless responses from her with each touch of his capable hands. There will, however, be the odd occasion when the raw animalistic nature of his lovemaking will seem a little rough and ready for the refined tastes of this Libra lady, just as the Aries man will feel that it's a bit of a nuisance waiting for her to set the scene for sex and seduction when he just wants to get on with it. She's too polite to object, but after he had praised her gorgeous, delectable body, it would have been more respectful of him to have seductively removed her pristine silk lingerie first.

LIBRA WOMAN WITH **TAURUS MAN**

 In love: It is in the Taurus man that the Libra woman finds a partner who will appreciate her talents and refined behavior. The Libra woman has an innate appreciation for all fine things and her attractive appearance says it all. The Taurus man will easily develop a love of and appreciation for everything that she stands for. He'll be romantic, never forgetting her birthday or anniversary, and candlelit dinners for two will be a regular feature of their relationship. He is, of course, entranced by her effortless femininity and by the way she always asks him for his opinion and considers his feelings before making a decision. She, in her turn, will be intrigued by his ability to relate to her feminine qualities: he will go shopping with her and offer opinions on female issues without finding these things threatening to his masculinity—which underlines that masculinity even more. He adores being made to feel as if he's the epitome of strength and manliness, just as she loves the feeling of peace and safety he gives her. It's a relationship that has all the elements of togetherness that they both yearn for. Both signs are ruled by the planet Venus, so love, beauty, and art are powerful motivating forces in their lives. Their shared abode would be a sumptuous symphony of good taste and comfort: the eye would delight in its harmonious play of color, texture, and light. Taureans can be stubborn though, so there may be times when the Libra woman will have to rely heavily on her skills of diplomacy.

 In bed: Bed is where this couple differs, and the differences could either be looked upon as enjoyable, enlightening, and erotic, or as something that finally rubs both of them up the wrong way— literally. Making love means very different things to each of them, but both are pretty willing to please, so making adjustments to suit the other will certainly keep a smile on their faces for some time afterward! Friends and family will wonder what's going on! The Taurus man is sensual and earthy, with a powerful need for physical contact. She is airy, and enjoys indulging in the fantasy realm of romantic ideals. What turns her on is not only the gentle touch of his hands on her body, but the meeting of minds and quest for poetic love expressed through whispered words. However, her desire for a mental union may leave him a little bewildered, just as his purely physical approach may have her shying away. "Surely he loves me for my mind?" cries the Libra lady. "Can't she see how much I love her by the way I'm longing to get her into bed?" bemoans the Taurus man. This is where the whole loved-up Venusian relationship can fall apart, but since they're both creative, it's unlikely to do so. Feeding strawberries dipped in chocolate to one another while lying in bed will help spur on the process of getting it on, and the heat will rapidly rise from this point onward!

LiBRA WOMAN WiTH GEMiNi MAN

In love: The Gemini man and Libra woman will be flitting around each other like a couple of hummingbirds looking for, and finding, sweet nectar. Both delight in being around someone who possesses the same bright and airy approach to life as they do. The Libra woman, who loves to make a mental connection, will never run out of things to say to Mr. Gemini, and he'll hang on her every word. Many a dawn will break before either of them tire of their scintillating conversations, though, because they are so much on the same wavelength, there will also be times when words won't be necessary. It's true that the erratic and restless Gemini could throw Lady Libra's world out of balance, but she finds his energy so irresistible that somehow it doesn't seem to matter that much to her. An uncertain future with him is better than a future without him. The practicalities of life will definitely get in the way of their bliss but time apart will only make their longing and love for one another grow. Her effortless grace, elegance, and charm captivate and hold this man's normally wandering attention, so he'll no longer have such a great need to do his own thing, at least not without his Libra woman by his side. She brings out his desire to create something magical for the both of them. There is such a natural affinity between the Libra woman and Gemini man that they'll never be seriously distracted when in each other's company. There's lots of honey where this relationship comes from.

 In bed: When a Libra woman tells a Gemini man her sexual fantasies, he thrills at the way they reflect his own and will do everything in his power to indulge her and make them real. Even if he doesn't quite get it right, they'll both end up giggling and rolling around the bedroom so much that lovemaking will be a truly joyous event. When he brushes his dexterous fingers over her body, she exudes a soft sweetness that is an exquisite invitation for him to do more, go farther, and fly higher. Both of them have a vision in their mind of the ideal romantic union expressed in a sexy, sensual storm that sweeps them along on the wings of erotic passion. The unbearable lightness of being that can exist when these two wrap their bodies around each other brings them closer to that vision than either could hope for. The climactic moment is often reached at the same time, and together they will float high in the divine light of heavenly bliss. He propels her into these stratospheres of pleasure and she'll stay with him all the way, while she brings him higher than he ever thought possible. Such is the strength of this loving union that they easily become one, which is a major feat for the dualistic Gemini man. What are the pitfalls? Sooner or later, one or both of them will have to get out of bed and get dressed if they are to pay the bills.

LIBRA WOMAN WITH CANCER MAN

 In love: Cancer man's gentleness and sensitivity make it easy for the Libra lady to love him. She is naturally drawn to his refined manner and he is immediately intrigued by her delicate beauty. Both enjoy surrounding themselves with beautiful things, so homemaking will be a shared pleasure. At first glance, it looks as if Mr. Crab is the man the Libra lady has been looking for, and together they can make a real love nest. If she's ever feeling blue, he'll wrap his arms snugly around her, but he's also happy to go along for the ride when her spirits are high. That is, unless he's in one of his dark moods and she's in one of her flirty phases—perhaps flirting with one of his friends. He won't just sit there and take it. He'll be vocal in his displeasure until she may feel as though she's drowning in a sea of his emotions. At these times they simply won't connect. He'll be demanding reassurance and wanting to be mothered, just when she's in the mood to go out and party! Their relationship can sometimes be downright difficult, sometimes deliriously delightful. In other words, it won't always be harmonious but it won't be hellish either. Such is the changeable nature of Libra and the moodiness of Cancer when they're together. At best, they'll have a beautifully dynamic partnership. At worst, it could become a competition to see who's better at making the other one feel guilty. Unless they're both winners, both will lose out.

 In bed: The sexual side of the Cancer man and Libra woman relationship begins long before these two get between the sheets. It starts when she flutters her eyelashes at him and he "accidentally" brushes his hand across her breast. They'll titillate and tease one another into a heightened state of desire to make sure that the other is fully committed before getting undressed. Once they're actually in bed, the sexual experience for the Cancer man and Libra lady involves a lot of ups and downs. Get ready to get emotional. This man can make such beautiful love that she could end up crying with the sweetness of it. And he's not afraid of her tears; in fact, he'll adore her even more for her display of emotion. However, there could sometimes be a conflict between her need for light and easy lovemaking and his for a deeper connection. It's a roller-coaster ride that's both scary and fun. It will be a moving experience, one way or another, and he won't be quick to let go when she wants to get off, which means that the next round of tears could be caused by something altogether different.

LIBRA WOMAN WITH **LEO MAN**

 In love: Every time the Leo man looks at her, the Libra woman feels a lovely warm glow spreading from her heart right through to her fingertips. She immediately connects with his romantic chivalry; it makes her heart do backflips. The Leo man really appreciates her sense of style and her refined good taste, and he feels that it reflects well on him that she's so graceful and captivating. He'll want to indulge her every desire. All Lady Libra has to do is worship the ground her Leo man walks on—and she probably will! When it comes to parties and work occasions, he'll look dignified and she'll complement him perfectly, which is just as he would want. She has a great sense of etiquette and knowledge of the social graces, so he'll be proud to take her everywhere he goes. He needs her vision and broad intellect while she just loves his dynamism. Together they make a bright and lively couple. This man wants to be the center of her universe, which shouldn't be a problem for the relationship-loving Libra lady, but she might find it a little draining to have to continually massage such a super-huge ego. She may also have to tone down any flirtatious tendencies she feels, otherwise she'll be the cause of his frequent and unpleasant displays of jealousy. But his loyalty and her need for partnership are likely to result in real commitment. Put love into the equation, and this becomes a sublime match.

In bed: This is one sexy man! What's more, he's charismatic and possesses the kind of animal magnetism that comes from a powerful self-confidence and the belief that he's truly special. The Libra woman should have no trouble luring the Lion into her bedroom and capturing his heart. She's like a sweet honey-trap that will make him throw caution to the wind. Her idealized way of lovemaking is to shower the bed with rose petals and massage him with exotic-smelling oils; he'll respond to this with raunchy fieriness. He'll turn her on with one single touch and his unrestrained passion will keep her feeling alive all night long. She'll show such willing excitement in his arms that he won't be able to get enough of her, but she also likes to make a mental connection with her lover, so the two of them may have to take the occasional break in order to fulfill her need for some verbal erotic fantasy. Once he sees how much this heightens her arousal, the Leo man will be generous with his sexy pillow talk. At first, she may have to try to decipher his growling sounds, but once she gets used to his deeply erotic ways, she'll find him easier to understand. She could try to slow him down by speaking slowly and sensually. She'll know when he's ready to burst!

LIBRA WOMAN WITH VIRGO MAN

 In love: The Libra lady won't even realize when the Virgo man draws her in. He's so subtle and she's so susceptible to his charm. He appeals to her mind; in fact, he will show her from the start that he loves her way of thinking. She can wax lyrical with him and he'll listen, encouraging her and paying her the compliments that she really needs to hear. She just knows that there's more to him than meets the eye. There's a genuinely loving compatibility between these two: they'll never have to remind each other to pick up their dirty socks from the floor, for example! He finds her charm and grace irresistible and can hardly wait to get her on her own, but sometimes they'll get so bound up in discussing ideals and the way things should be, that they never actually get around to making things happen between them. The Libra lady is idealistic and aims high, while he wants to win the world for her—unfortunately this isn't really within the realms of possibility, so there could be some disappointment. So long as they both want the same things out of life, they'll find in each other a supporting partner, but the moment their goals differ, then things may go pear-shaped. Although she'll appear to take his criticisms with good grace and will make the necessary adjustments, if there's one thing out of balance about a Libra lady, then she'll shift the burden of blame right back in his direction and he'll find he's made a rod for his own back.

 In bed: The Virgo man loves sex—pure, perfect sex. The Libra lady is one purring sex kitten—she definitely won't be able to stop herself from rubbing up against him. This is the man who'll simply adore seeing the loving Libra lady dressed in virginal lacy white lingerie and she will no doubt be happy to oblige. It will appeal both to her fantasy notions of romance and to his libido if she lies invitingly on the bed, looking like a work of art while he studies every inch of her with his artisan eyes and touches her with his deft craftsman fingers. He's earthy, real, and thorough as well as sensually switched on, so he'll do anything she needs. He'll quickly find that his ability to focus his efforts fully on the little things brings very satisfactory results. She'll never leave him high and dry, and though what he offers her may not be spiritual or even emotional, it will certainly be stimulating in all the right places. He gets to her on the physical level and she gets to him on the mental level. He likes the fact that she's rather vocal and enjoys telling him her fantasies almost as much as she likes the clever way he makes his actions fit her words.

LIBRA WOMAN WITH **LIBRA MAN**

 In love: As with many things connected to Libra, this relationship can have one of two outcomes. It can be beautifully romantic with each adoring the other in a very chocolates-and-roses kind of way. They'll leave each other sweet notes signed and sealed with a kiss, even when they're only popping out to the grocery store. But the other way things can pan out is like a seesaw—up and down, with both constantly striving to find the middle. But oh! Once they've found that equilibrium, how perfectly lovely things become! They'll chirp away like a pair of lovebirds. Their conversations will range wide and deep, they'll never be bored with each other and, if they do disagree, they'll always make allowances for the other's point of view. This relationship always has its rose-tinted spectacles on. They find it romantic and charming just to be in each other's company and they're so considerate of one another that neither will make any plans without first consulting the other. This relationship is bound to work unless one of the two takes a flirt with someone else a little too far. Then it's a case of what's sauce for the goose is sauce for the gander; both will become way too competitive, and as far as extra-curricular activities go, that's just altogether too much sauce.

 In bed: The up-and-down seesaw dynamic that exists between the Libra couple makes for a swinging time in bed! When the timing is right, they'll enjoy a languorous and deliciously sweet experience between the sheets. Both will have found the perfect person for the projection of all their fantasies and, since each is the other's ideal, they won't want to miss out on gazing at the real thing so they'll be happy to leave the lights on. The more they whisper sweet nothings in each other's ear, the more their passions will rise. They'll have the scent of delicious perfume wafting through the air to make them drunk with pleasure, and they'll tantalize one another to dizzying heights of anticipation in the most delicately erotic way. But the whole sexual episode may take a while to set up because they're rather fussy about getting the mood right before they indulge their refined romantic tastes. If they can't have rose petals on a bed surrounded by candles, or soft music playing in the background, then they'll talk each other through a thought-provoking fantasy instead. Either way, they require a long preparation time. Of course, the end result has them gliding along at such stratospheric levels of bliss that they'll always believe it was worth it.

LIBRA WOMAN WITH **SCORPIO MAN**

In love: The Scorpio man really loves a challenge and he knows just how he's going to get his Libra woman—or so he thinks. He'll go after her single-mindedly, using some of the most thrilling seduction techniques that she's ever encountered, but she's pretty savvy when it comes to one-on-one tricks and will be completely clued in on what he's up to. She certainly likes it, but is perhaps not so sure that she wants it. Maybe at first she just enjoys playing hard to get, or maybe she senses that she could be going down a seriously dangerous route with this guy, because his version of one-on-one tricks is a bit more grown-up than her own. The Scorpio man knows what he wants and he likes what he sees on the surface. He'll assume that there's a lot more to uncover, but he might not get what he expects! The question the Libra woman will keep asking herself is, does she have what it takes to keep him interested? The answer is, probably, but what she should be asking herself is, does she want to keep him interested? Scorpio man can be very manipulative and there's a chance that the Libra lady might not like the way he wants to mold her. There's an undeniable attraction between these two but they also have a few sticking points to get over first. As long as they get stuck on each other and don't get stuck on those contentious points, then this is a mutually fascinating love affair that could last and last.

In bed: The Scorpio man loves to get right up close and personal and when it comes to sex, that's his mission statement. He'll manipulate his way right to his Libra lady's most sensitive spots. He's also a man who likes to be on top, and in more ways than one! He may try a variety of techniques in order to elicit some reaction from her, but though she's the mistress of reactions, he might not quite understand how that necessitates her giving a running commentary on the experience and verbalizing all the sexy thoughts that are running through her head. If he allows Lady Libra to take the lead, dark and dangerous Scorpio man might find her bright and breezy approach to lovemaking a little too light for his tastes, although he always finds playing the villain to her damsel in distress quite a turn-on. His sexual appetites run deeper than she may be prepared to go, for her natural tendency is to soar beyond any purely physical sensuality. If she gives him a chance, then he could seduce her around to his way of thinking. He's hot, tasty, and truly masterful at creating erotic tension, so it would be hard for the Libra lady not to succumb to his advances. Then she'll melt in his embrace and know that she's in for a really rocking time.

LIBRA WOMAN WITH **SAGITTARIUS MAN**

 In love: The Sagittarius man will sweep the Libra woman off her feet, take her on a whirlwind ride and then, hey! Where did he go? But he'll be back, for he sees all that's lovely in her. The problem is that he sees loveliness everywhere and can't help but go and take a closer look! However, when this man commits, he does so wholeheartedly, unlike the Lady Libra, who'll still be weighing up the pros and cons in the relationship until well after the marriage. But she loves him; he has a refined soul and a touch of wildness that thrills and excites her, and he also makes her laugh and feel free to express her true self. He might not always take her views into consideration when he's making a decision and although she'd like him to, he certainly doesn't tell her that he loves her every five minutes. But she knows he does without him telling her, so, to keep the peace that she wants and needs, it's better for her to let him think he has all the freedom in the world. And if he thinks he has, then he'll show her that what he really wants is her! It's true that he suffers from wanderlust and always will, but when he's around, he's so appreciative of all her good qualities that she doesn't mind. And after all, when she stops to think about it, his wanderlust suits the sociable Libra lady perfectly because that leaves her free to spend time with friends, and do a little flirting—which only serves to keep her keen on her Sagittarius man since she'll find that he really is one in a million.

 In bed: This is an energetic relationship—in the bedroom, in the bathroom, in the kitchen, on the stairs, in the garden, on the way home….Things can get hot and heavy between the Libra lady and the Sagittarius man just about anytime and anywhere, though "hot and happy" might be a better description, for they just have so much fun frolicking about in the bedroom. When she shows him her bright, bubbly side, he can't help but get extremely excited and then there's no stopping him. He won't hold back for nicety's sake and he may not have all the refined, romantic qualities that she desires in a lover, but he's certainly adventurous and so fantastically frisky that his spontaneous streak could catch her unawares at the most awkward moments. But the rough-and-ready Sagittarius man won't mind; in fact he finds her unpreparedness a real turn-on. It brings out the beast in him and makes him wild with passion. Of course, she'll try to tame him, but she's no match for his passion—he'll hunt her down and turn her on beyond the point of no return.

LIBRA WOMAN WITH **CAPRICORN MAN**

 In love: In many ways, the Libra woman and the Capricorn man were made for each other. Given time, the things that they have in common will help them achieve a very comfortable lifestyle. Both are ambitious and, to some extent, share the same refinement of taste and the same standards. However, if they're not careful about the things that they don't agree on, this relationship could result in tension and discomfort for them both. The Capricorn man finds the lovely Libra lady very attractive; he appreciates her mind just as much as he appreciates the attention that she pays to her appearance. He'll want to capture her and pin her down, but is it ever possible to pin down a delicate butterfly without doing some damage? She wants to be in a committed relationship, one where she can talk about and share the ideals and fantasies that her man has for the two of them. She'll love his sense of responsibility and the stability he offers but at times, she might find him too down-to-earth to be a dreamer and this could be a real downer to her lightheartedness. Of course, he does have dreams, big dreams, but he's much too coolly practical ever to express them out loud until he's fairly certain that achieving them is well within his grasp. Unfortunately, that could be too late for her. However, there's a powerful energy when these two are together; it's both exciting and a little scary. Their love won't flow easily but it will certainly be intense.

 In bed: It has to be said that the sensual Capricorn man is a really randy Goat! He wants the Libra lady and she knows it! He won't be satisfied with fantasy foreplay—flirty, teasing conversations or chasing her around the bedroom to build up her excitement levels. He needs physical contact, and lots of it! It's always good when they get going but she shouldn't expect him to wait for her to be in the mood. She needs to be able to supply sex on demand—and he'll be demanding it all the time! The Capricorn man simply isn't capable of watching her move gracefully across the room without having a powerful physical reaction, but who would ever have guessed it from his sober-looking exterior? Well, Lady Libra will know it by the way he devours her with his eyes. They may be out to dinner, for example, and he'll suddenly get the urge. He only has to give her one look and she'll not only be blushing, she'll be squirming with eagerness. But they'll have to contain themselves until they get home because the public restrooms won't provide either of them with the atmosphere they need! And that's when the randy Goat really needs to watch his step because, although she was all for it in the restaurant, by the time they get home her sexual scales may have tipped slightly out of balance. If he charges her into the bedroom before he's got her libido going again, then neither of them will get the satisfaction that they crave.

LIBRA WOMAN WITH **AQUARIUS MAN**

 In love: Since both of these people were born under Air signs, this is one very stimulating relationship. These two could sit and shoot the breeze together until the cows come home. The Aquarius man may not be the most romantic guy in the world, but he's zany and funny and the Libra lady finds him very attractive. He's also extremely receptive to her romantic ideals, because she doesn't load them with a heap of sticky emotions that would make him feel uncomfortable. At first, he connects with her on the level of friendship and although she may have to lead him up Lover's Lane, he'll certainly be fascinated enough to follow. She'll never be in any doubt that he finds her infatuating, and once she has grabbed his attention, she'll find that it's completely focused on every little thing she does. The Libra lady loves to talk and conceptualize and the Aquarius man loves it just as much, so these two can get into some really good conversations, exploring all the fabulous ideas that occur to them. He may sometimes take the high moral ground and try to tell her how to think, but she's clever enough to get her own point across. They'll both be totally delighted with the knowledge that, in loving one another, they've also found a friend for life. There exists a level of comfort and compatibility between these two lovers that simply can't be experienced by ordinary earthlings. This lucky couple will really hit it off and probably never have to come down from their clouds again.

 In bed: The Aquarius man is inventive—the Libra lady might even say a little kinky—but that shouldn't give her pause because here's a guy who'll listen to the fantasies that she whispers in his ear and will make them come true. She'll tell him that it's only with him that she wants to act out her fantasies, and that will really get him going! He needs her to flirt with him before he'll make a move, but since she loves to flirt that won't be a problem. Though she won't have the same quantity of romps with Mr. Aquarius as with some other men, she'll certainly have quality! Sometimes he'll do things to her that she didn't even think were possible, let alone sexy, while at other times he'll get her in the mood on the phone while he's on his way home, and then get distracted and not come back for hours. But she probably won't mind because, in the meantime, she'll either have been on the phone to someone else and will have forgotten all about his little telephone tease, or she'll have accepted an invitation to meet up with a friend instead. If she's really missing him then she should check out his toy cupboard. If he happens to walk in and catch her, then the games really will begin, for this guy can give a truly electrifying performance.

LiBRA WOMAN WiTH PiSCES MAN

 In love: These two share a dreamy kind of love and are captivated by a sense of romance and mystery. At last they've found an idealist like themselves, someone who longs for the same merging of mind and soul, all of which adds to the element of perfection in their relationship; they reach the point where they are completely at peace and in love with one another. The Pisces man will have the Libra lady believing his tales of make-believe so that they'll soon be imagining themselves floating on heavenly clouds, wrapped in gossamer-light robes, and listening to beautiful, other-worldly music. But hang on! Back on earth, in the real world, things aren't quite as magical as that! At times, Lady Libra could find herself walking on eggshells around this very sensitive man, especially when she pulls him up on one of his many unkept promises, and that can get a little draining for both of them. He means well, it's just that the fantasy feels better than the reality. While he wants to express their connection in an emotional manner, that's a bit too wishy-washy for her. Her preference is for an accord based on verbally expressed ideas, but no matter how flowery the language, he finds that too dry. He might feel under pressure in a relationship with the Libra lady and may end up floating off on one of those fluffy clouds all on his own. He shouldn't be surprised, though, when he looks back, to see her fanning the wind to help speed his departure.

In bed: The Pisces man can whip up a real-life fantasy in bed faster than Aunt Jemima can whip up a round of pancakes. All the Libra lady needs to do is to tell him one of her sexy stories and he'll catch her drift and turn it into a fast-moving current of sexual passion. That's when the Pisces man comes alive. He's so seductive and what's so sweet is that he doesn't seem at all sure of himself. He'll make love to her and make her feel loved like she's never been loved before and he'll immerse himself totally in her romantic fantasies, then turn them up a notch on the sex-o-meter. But there's one small catch—she shouldn't expect to be allowed up for air! He'll be in for the duration and she'll know it. He truly wants to lose himself in her, with no holds barred and no time limit. But if the Libra lady doesn't respond in the totally involved way that the shy Pisces man needs her to, then he'll probably droop over her like a wet blanket. This is such a shame for both of them because nothing turns a Libra lady off faster than feeling the weight of emotion bearing down on her when all she wants is to be lifted to the heights of erotic bliss. She's an enigma and it's not easy for him to get a real grip on her.

THE **LIBRA MAN** IN LOVE

The Libra man is always in love, and whether he's in love with the idea of love or with a real live person, it makes no difference to him because he behaves in exactly the same way. And that way is beautifully. His courtship manners are usually impeccable; for example, if he says he's going to call, he'll call and he'll be on time or even a little early, and then it will be to arrange a proper date. He enjoys the early stages of romancing a lover very much; he's flirty, charming, and a bit naughty, and although he has trouble making up his mind, he's actually more interested in the end product, the committed relationship. If he believes that a certain romantic liaison has no chance of going anywhere, he will gently, and so as not to cause offence, withdraw his attention. He would never be so callous as to deliberately hurt a lady's feelings.

Thanks to his idealized view of beauty he's rather partial to a pretty face and will often choose looks over other, more enduring qualities, but he also likes his woman to be bright and intelligent. A pretty, lively girl wearing an elegant outfit and a lovely smile is sure to capture his attention and his affection, and the Libra man won't complain if she isn't quite ready when he arrives to pick her up; he understands the finer points of applying makeup and the amount of effort it takes to get her hair into that unkempt, windswept look. He appreciates the pride she takes in her appearance and will love having her on his arm as he escorts her to fashionable restaurants and swanky parties. And she'd better be adept at the social graces, too, for when they're at a party, the Libra man enjoys flitting around, chatting here and flirting there, and while he'll be attentive to her needs and will let everyone know that they're an item, he won't put up with her acting resentful, jealous, or clingy.

When they're alone together he wants to talk—about them, about the other people they know, and about the ins and outs of their relationship. He longs to forge a mental union, where he and his lover are in perfect agreement about their roles in the partnership and about where they want to go as a couple. And as long as he continues to envisage a glittering future for the two of them, then he's happy, but he's not very good at doing the practical stuff that's needed to turn the dream into reality. He won't have any trouble buying her flowers and paying her compliments; he'll be totally reasonable and willing to compromise when any disagreements crop up between them; and he'll invest all his mental energy in finding solutions to the problems that they encounter, but she may have difficulty seeing if he's really invested his heart in the relationship. Displaying his emotions makes him uncomfortable and he'll resist any effort on her part to get him to react to her with real feeling. He'd rather run away and think his lofty thoughts, suppressing his emotions until he can understand them fully. But because what he lacks in ability to show intense depth of feeling he makes up for by being the epitome of the chivalrous romantic hero, it makes it pretty easy for a woman to turn a blind eye.

LiBRA man WiTH **ARiES WOMAN**

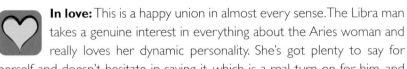 **In love:** This is a happy union in almost every sense. The Libra man takes a genuine interest in everything about the Aries woman and really loves her dynamic personality. She's got plenty to say for herself and doesn't hesitate in saying it, which is a real turn-on for him, and is something he could learn from her. She's impressed by his effortless charm and stimulating mind, both of which he uses to capture her attention. As opposites in the zodiac, the two of them make one whole. Each has what the other is missing. On occasion her impetuosity is a little too brash for his refined taste, just as his endless deliberating can have the Aries woman tapping her foot in irritation. But the longer these two hang around each other, the more they find things to adore and be thankful for in their relationship. At some point, they may really begin to meld and start taking after one another. Finishing one another's sentences will not be a source of irritation. Instead, it will be a comfort to be so thoroughly in tune with someone else. Both enjoy the excitement of a new challenge and neither is content to sit around waiting for life to come to them. Their mutually absorbing existence brings this couple into the realms of heavenly rapture.

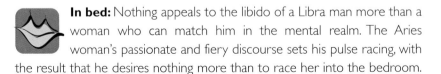 **In bed:** Nothing appeals to the libido of a Libra man more than a woman who can match him in the mental realm. The Aries woman's passionate and fiery discourse sets his pulse racing, with the result that he desires nothing more than to race her into the bedroom.

She'll be delighted by the way he responds to every move she makes. The more he feels her pleasure, the more he will give himself over to the whole experience. This girl doesn't know the meaning of holding back and nor will he once she invites him in. Their lovemaking reaches the parts that other mere sexual indulgences cannot reach. In fact, he'll reach parts of her that she didn't even know she had. And all because he knows the lady loves it. His cool, refined Libra persona and her unbridled desire and passion will create a special kind of chemistry between them. Here is a man who is as restless as the Aries woman. Neither will be able to sit still for long in the company of the other, and neither will want to. This is a "rock 'n' roll" match in every sense. These two will forever be captivated by the prospect of exploring each other's depths.

LIBRA MAN WITH **TAURUS WOMAN**

 In love: Venus, the planet of love, rules both Taurus and Libra, but each sign approaches love in a different way. Her approach is mental, his is physical. And the odds are against them because the elements of Earth (her) and Air (him) are not normally compatible, but with Venus uniting them, these problems can be transcended. Whatever happens, their ultimate aim is the same—love in its purest sense. If the Taurus woman and Libra man manage to achieve this, they'll find that the bond between them is as if sealed with a kiss from Aphrodite herself. What better blessing could there be? Their hearts can fly on the wings of love. However, it has to be said that the Libra man is a notorious flirt; he adores engaging women in scintillating conversation and delights in seeing the effect his charm has on them being reflected back at him from their eyes. This is very likely to cause the love he shares with Taurus to fly far away unless it gets the grounding that the Taurus woman can instill into the relationship. She's jealous and possessive, but much too controlled to fly into a rage. What is more likely to happen is that because she's hurt and confused by his behavior, she'll erect a wall between them to protect her vulnerability. Unless he's able to break it down quickly, he may find that wall getting so high and impenetrable that not even Aphrodite, the goddess of love, can bring about its destruction.

 In bed: Soft, sensuous, and romantic, the bedroom experience between the Taurus woman and Libra man will be like something from a storybook—or perhaps more like an erotic novel. It will be a tasteful treat in more ways than one. These Venus-ruled signs are into quality. From the atmospheric décor and scented candles to the carefully chosen fine champagne, this experience will appeal to the esthetic sense of both of them. They really know how to enjoy themselves and, equally, how to please one another, despite their different approaches. The Taurus woman will enthuse the Libra man with her slow, steady movement, while the Libra man will excite the Taurus woman with his ability to move from one pleasure zone to another. They'll want to explore each other's forbidden fruits and will happily make a meal of it, but no knives and forks please—only bite-sized portions. The only problem facing this passionate pairing is his need for more than just a physical expression of togetherness. His intimacy must be one of the mind as well as the body. She, on the other hand, converses best through touch; her language is that of the caress. They may end up facing a communication breakdown that's impossible to fix.

LIBRA MAN WITH **GEMINI WOMAN**

 In love: When the Gemini woman and Libra man get together, a magical thing happens: they present each other's best side to the rest of the world. They'll be on everyone's A-list for dinner parties because together they are the pinnacle of sophistication, refined taste, beauty, charm, and wit. Their conversation flows with intelligence and articulation. Mentally, they just click; they've really got it. There's lots of laughing and loving, jesting and teasing between these two, and the world just seems a lighter, brighter place when they are around. When they are alone together all the magic is turned on the other. The Gemini woman is helplessly seduced by the elegant, eloquent, clever Libra brain—he can romance her with just a look and a word—while she will intrigue and impress him with her quick-thinking ability to grasp all his serious conceptual ideas, and will constantly surprise him with her amusing, playful banter. The only problem that these two lovers might face is that they both find it practically impossible to make up their minds about almost anything. But that's all right because they love each other's company so much and have all the time in the world to decide on whether they should buy this sofa or that, live here or there, or go north or south on vacation. But, once they've made a decision, they'll grow old together and never tire of one another. This is certainly one of those matches that are made in heaven. Life will be eternal bliss.

 In bed: For this couple, bed is their playground. It's where they'll linger on into the early hours with the most artful, tasteful, and romantic lovemaking ever. The Libra man really thrills when all his senses are tingling with desire. He adores the feel of beautiful lace against delicate silken sheets and he's a man who'll appreciate the natural softness of his Gemini lady. But he'll also buy the necessary accessories to play up her coquettish beauty—perfumed candles, scent, romantic music—and complete the perfect lovemaking. These two both like to talk and it would amuse the rest of the world if they could hear the running commentary during one of their marathon sex sessions. What the Gemini woman has to say would go down well at any late-night risqué comedy club, while her Libra man could make a small fortune in the romantic greeting cards business. But these two are unlikely ever to write their material down because they're so caught up in just being together. Each time they glance at one another, excitement flutters in their hearts, their breathing gathers pace, and everything feels fresh and new, just like the first thrilling time they came together. Born under the sign of the Scales, the Libra man knows how to get the balance right and is ever aware of the importance of sharing and the nature of give and take. These fanciful, romantic lovers will have each other reeling in ecstasy.

LIBRA MAN WITH CANCER WOMAN

 In love: When the Libra man is in love, he's more charming and romantic than any prince in any fairytale. He's a gentleman in every possible respect and even if he's one of those rare gentlemen who are a little rough around the edges, he's never crude or uncouth. But despite all his romantic, captivating charm, the Cancer woman may not fall for him immediately because she's naturally cautious and, being rather enchanting herself, she knows just how irresistible a touch of fairy glamour can be. But should he ever make up his mind to pursue her, he'll woo her until she simply can't say "no." He'll treat her like a lady, opening doors for her and kissing her hand, and unless she's a militant feminist, she'll turn on her own beguiling charms, which will have a very powerful effect on him indeed. The one hurdle that he'll eventually have to jump with her concerns his fickleness and flirtatiousness. She needs to know that he'll be there for her, and being such an intuitive lady, she'll know whether or not he's serious. Meanwhile he, having been born under an Air sign, likes to be free as a bird, so her clingy tendencies could bring him down. On the whole, however, he's very attracted to the caring, comforting, and nurturing femininity of her character, and her shifting emotions add a touch of mystery that heightens the appeal. They will pursue one another with equal enthusiasm and, given time, could really grow to need the beautiful love that is played out between them.

In bed: Libra is ruled by the amorous planet Venus, so it's sweet all through. As a result, the Libra man is hard to resist; he's a smooth-talking, heart-stopping love machine. He knows perfectly well how to make the Cancer woman go weak at the knees. However, the most powerful ingredient in this sexual union is love. If they are to find happiness in each other's arms, love is absolutely essential to both of them. A randy romp around the bedroom might be fun but they'll end up feeling empty and even a bit lonely. There's potential for variety here, however; a few randy romps alternating with some romantic candlelit trysts will keep them both turned on. The Libra man's need for beauty, harmony, immaculately clean sheets, and fantasy to whet his sexual appetite are things she can be sensitive to, but these won't always give her the feelings of closeness that are so important to her. But where there's a will, there's a way, and once they've caught the other's sexual drift, they'll always be willing to go all the way.

LiBRA MAN WiTH **LEO WOMAN**

 In love: The Leo woman loves being fussed over and the Libra man is capable of really making her feel like a queen. She will, of course, reward him generously for his attentive adoration. He'll woo her in the most romantic and gallant style, and she'll find it near impossible to resist his charms. When he proposes to her, he'll be down on one knee with the most beautiful ring that she has ever seen, for he knows exactly what she likes—nothing but the best! He's into esthetic beauty so he'll love the way the Leo lady's always picture-perfect and he respects her dignified principles. She believes that one must always look poised; he agrees and will be there at her side in his slick designer suit. They love this about one another but theirs isn't just a mutual appreciation society; they are both also very sociable people and it does their relationship a power of good that everyone regards them as an attractive, glittering beacon to crowd around. Their love may be their own exclusive, personal pleasure, but it radiates from them and has an uplifting, positive effect on their friends. As long as they're together, their home will be a lively, interesting, fun place to be.

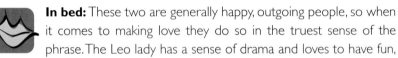 **In bed:** These two are generally happy, outgoing people, so when it comes to making love they do so in the truest sense of the phrase. The Leo lady has a sense of drama and loves to have fun, so she's full of surprises: she might turn up at dinnertime in just lacy lingerie or a gossamer negligée! The Libra man will quickly see exactly what she has in mind, gently kissing her hand, then nibbling his way up her arm to reach her outstretched neck. She'll be full of anticipation and he won't let her down. This couple's antics could make a tantalizingly naughty story, but they prefer to act it out. He's a very active lover, so when the Leo lady is in one of her lazier moods, she won't miss out on any pleasure. He'll admire her body and tease her with his light, exciting touch. When she's fired up, no man could be more excited than the Libra man she's with. She gives him a reason to be a man and he's thrilled by the thought of having such a glorious woman wanting his body.

LiBRA man WiTH VIRGO WOMAN

In love: The Libra man is gifted with intelligence so he recognizes and admires the Virgo woman's mental agility. This makes for a strong initial attraction—they'll feel compelled to pick each other's brains for personal facts and general opinions. He's charming, clean, and well-dressed, and he's extremely pleased that she's always picture-perfect and takes such a pride in her appearance. One thing that's certain about this couple is that their life will run smoothly; their bills will always be paid on time, and their lovely home will never be untidy or be allowed to fall down around their ears. They work well together to make a pleasing environment where they can settle down and enjoy one another's company. The Libra man will accommodate his Virgo woman's need to analyze his psyche and he will find her modesty sweet and alluring. She'll be impressed by his refined, affable character and lofty ideas. This could be a perfect, mutually appreciative relationship—if only there were some spark! But that's not to say that it won't work. With so much that's right between these two lovers, it can't be wrong; simply ask Mr. Libra. He's already weighing up the pros and cons. No relationship is ever perfect but since these signs are next to one another in the zodiac, there's bound to be more than enough overlap to keep this couple running in a fuel-efficient mode for the rest of their lives. There's not much drama here, but who needs it when they can take the easy road together?

In bed: If the Virgo woman and Libra man were to start talking about how they would like to make love, it would certainly be a fun way to rev up their sexual motors. Both of them get very aroused by ideas, so the seduction could take place in their heads, which is titillating because of its ambiguity. Once her engine is ready, she'll find out if he can live up to his promises, but if she's left idling for too long, her excitement could turn into her doubting her own attractiveness. Things could stall at this point but he'll be ready to give it a jump-start if they do. Did he really need to head back to the kitchen, though, for the champagne and scented candles before climbing between the sheets? She should be flattered that he goes to so much trouble to make it a beautiful experience, so does she really need to criticize him? Unfortunately, by her interpretation, it wasn't her needs that she saw him being attentive to, but his own. And she was so looking forward to attending to him in her own way. There's room here for both to fix things!

LIBRA MAN WITH **LIBRA WOMAN**

See pages 66–67.

LIBRA MAN WITH **SCORPIO WOMAN**

In love: Thanks to their mutual desire to connect with people on a personal level, the Libra man and Scorpio woman share some of the same feelings and views on life. Both know all the good things that there are about being in a relationship and they often also have a strong spiritual attraction. Her search for psychological understanding means that she appreciates his need to analyze their love life and get a more thorough knowledge of what makes it and her tick. His charm, backed up by brains, appeals to her penetrating mind and powerful femininity and she likes the impact that her attributes have on him. He really wants to be her guy, the one she turns to for everything, but her intuition tells her that he'll resist any intense, emotional expressions of feelings. He, meanwhile, finds it very difficult to convey what he feels in any way other than verbally. In short, he won't like her dragging out of him all the unpleasant things that he prefers to keep hidden. His light, flirty sociability can sometimes appear a little shallow to the Scorpio woman. For a while at least, this relationship can be a great voyage of discovery for the two of them, but for a more permanent arrangement, compromise is the key. That's easy enough for him but perhaps that's because he doesn't seem to care as much as she does.

 In bed: At times the Libra man will be everything a Scorpio woman could hope for in a lover. He's thoughtful, charming, and romantic, and he'll thoroughly enjoy setting the scene for their moments of sweet passion. His elegant seduction techniques will be great for building her anticipation. Candlelight, violins, bouquets of roses, and perfect sweet nothings whispered in her ear will have her in the mood for lovemaking more often than she'd be willing to admit. He's also open to her suggestions, although he's so considerate and so enjoys making her feel good that she'd be hard-pressed to find ways for him to improve. Scorpio lady's sexiness inspires commitment to the pleasures of the flesh. To begin with, it's her powerful sensuality that attracts him, but after his first experience of sliding between the sheets with her, he'll just want to keep coming back for more. She's so sexually intuitive that she's able to control their connection, while he goes deeper and more compellingly into things, and that can unleash a storm of feelings. This is dangerous territory for him; he finds it highly exciting but, in the end, he just might not be able to match and sustain such deep levels of eroticism. They have slightly different styles, but if he takes his time in exploring those deep levels and brings along with him his sincere love for her, then the magic of their sexual chemistry will do its thing and, given time, the lovemaking will get more and more amazing for them both.

LiBRA mAn WiTH SAGiTTARiuS WOMAN

 In love: From the moment when they first meet, the Libra man will charm the Sagittarius lady. He'll see all that's exciting and beautiful in her, and will make it his mission to attract her attention so that he can tell her all about it. He'll wine and dine her and woo her with so much romanticism that she simply can't refuse him, and why would she? This man has everything she could ever want, and might even give her the earth if she asked for it. Even a more rough-and-ready Libra man will bring out her feminine side and make her feel like a heroine in a romantic novel. These two will enjoy being together at parties, in restaurants, walking along a moonlit beach, in the bedroom, anywhere. They have such an easygoing rapport that it seems as though there's something running through their blood that supplies them with enough action, fun, and adventure to keep their hearts burning with desire for one another. There'll be no temper tantrums or violent scenes between these two, because when they put their heads together, they can work out almost any problem. Except perhaps one: the Sagittarius woman needs the freedom to come and go as she pleases, while the Libra man needs the two of them to do everything together, so he might want to tag along even when it's not appropriate. Love and friendship come easily to these two and it can be a long-lived and ideal partnership as long as they keep the channels of communication open.

 In bed: At first, the Sagittarius woman's lovemaking is free and easy, and bright and breezy, but the more she warms up, the more wild and abandoned she becomes. The Libra man is very giving and wants her to have a good a time, so he'll do all he can to fan her flame into a passionate inferno, while she could be just the *femme fatale* he needs to ignite a fire in him that he never knew he had! He more than responds to her adventurous, lusty expression of sexuality; it makes him feel as though he's riding high on love when the Lady Centaur looks at him with burning desire in her eyes. She'll carry him far beyond the edge of his expectations. He's had the fantasy, now here's the real thing! But she must behave in a ladylike fashion, which is not always easy for a woman whose unleashed passion can make her howl like the wildest of animals. And that's the only catch in this coupling; he's all man and possesses a powerful libido, but he has romantic ideas about how love should be expressed. Although he likes his Sagittarius woman to be feral and free, he also wants her to be sweetly mysterious and feminine. That's a bit like asking a wild horse to take part in a dressage routine. If he wants to keep her, he'll need to find his inner animal to match hers.

LIBRA MAN WITH CAPRICORN WOMAN

In love: The Libra man and Capricorn lady both have a forward-looking approach to love and life. They have no problem putting in some effort in order to build up a relationship that will provide lasting commitment and scope for their ambitions. She loves his mind and is easily won over by his romantic gestures and his ability to discuss their relationship fascinates her. Meanwhile, he is impressed by her intensity and finds her cool demeanor very attractive. However, he'll drive her mad with his inability to make a decision without endless deliberation—that would wear down even the most patient Capricorn! She'd be delighted if he would simply stop talking about the relationship and start participating in it. He will also have to learn to make space for her occasional serious, brooding moods and not take them personally. They're both natural leaders and need the freedom to rule themselves, so she may even try to take control and make decisions for him, which he'll dislike intensely. The tension that can build up between them goes against their ideals of a happy union, so the relationship could be uncomfortable unless their other personal traits are compatible.

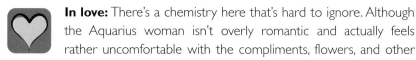

In bed: The Libra man just can't seem to make up his mind about whether the mood or timing is right, but with a little encouragement, he'll begin his seduction routine. It may take some time for him to decide whether to do this or that, but the Capricorn woman is patient and when he's done with all his romantic wooing and whispering of sexy scenarios in her ear, they'll both be ready to step things up a notch and to express their feelings physically. Once they get their gear off and get into bed, the tension and sexual energy between them is so tangible that it could be cut with a knife. But it seems a shame that it's such an ordeal getting there. Once they do, they'll throw themselves into their sexual satisfaction with a hunger that won't be sated before they've climbed some dizzy heights and become quite breathless from the exertion. She will respond to his tickling and teasing just as long as he can keep up with her stamina. If she takes the lead, he'll get so turned on by her enthusiasm and apparently insatiable desire for him that he'll immediately stop thinking and dive right in!

LiBRA mAn WiTH **AQUARiUS WOmAn**

In love: There's a chemistry here that's hard to ignore. Although the Aquarius woman isn't overly romantic and actually feels rather uncomfortable with the compliments, flowers, and other love tokens that are Mr. Libra's stock-in-trade, when he has her in his sights, this is a beautiful relationship. His way of expressing love is light and breezy, and expands her view of what love is all about. She also finds it refreshing because there are no strings attached. He'll captivate her so gently that she won't even notice it and no one else brings out the soft femininity of an Aquarius woman like he does. Her original, entertaining conversation inspires him to think in idealistic terms and she shows him how creative his fantasies could be. This is a love that starts in the mind, then moves into the heart. There will rarely be any harsh words between them, just a natural inclination to see the best in each other. However, if at times he's feeling off balance because of her lack of attachment, the only way he can right himself is to put her off balance, too, but she'll usually be able to cope pretty well with that. Life and love flow easily between these two, and as long as they can keep their flirty eyes from wandering, theirs should be a long-lived love affair.

 In bed: Sex between a Libra man and Aquarius woman is like a flight of fancy that's fueled by words of encouragement. He gets turned on by her bedroom banter—she speaks the unspeakable in the most gentle and seductive tones. When she tells him he's gorgeous, he'll devote hours to her pleasure. He also loves it when she dresses up, so she could slip into her white, silky lingerie and then, when she's done that, she could light some scented candles and whisper even more sweet, sensual nothings in his ear. He appreciates her inventive sexual storytelling more than most and gets excited by her original, erotic fantasies. He's spent so much time thinking about the most wonderful and perfect ways to do "it" that he finds it quite a turn-on to have someone come up with kinky new ideas that even he hasn't thought of. She, meanwhile, will be drawn in by the romantic wonder with which he expresses his love for her. That will push back even farther the boundaries of her vast imagination and will inspire her to do things that will make the hairs on his chest stand on end! Lovemaking between these two is smooth, sensual, and loving. This girl's famous for being detached but with a Libra man she can get very attached indeed.

LiBRA MAN WiTH **PiSCES WOMAN**

In love: The Libra man and Pisces woman could be the most heart-stoppingly romantic couple ever. They're equally loving and he's very good at doing all those little things that a girl expects from her partner. It's floating-away-on-gossamer-wings time, with harps serenading the happy couple as they drift up into paradise. These two will always remember the song that was playing when they first gazed at each other across a crowded room and they'll play it on anniversaries and when they feel romantic. Eventually, however, it will feel as if that song is the only thing keeping them together for, while he spends a lot of time thinking and talking about their relationship, she might be the only one who truly invests in it emotionally. They might not get what they need from each other unless she can play it cool and he can be a little more emotionally involved. That might be asking too much, despite the promising start to the relationship. However, their love is very real and there's no reason why it shouldn't last. It all depends on how they play it; if they stay in the now, the relationship could work, but they may not have the capacity to grow together as many couples do.

In bed: When it's time for a little lovin' with the lights down low, the Libra man wants everything to be perfect for his sweet Pisces lady. So that means a scented bubble bath followed by her putting on her silky lingerie. And she shouldn't forget to put her hair up; he's always wanted to do that thing where he takes the pins out and she shakes her head while looking up at him adoringly! She can certainly play this game of allure and the naughty little things he says and does to excite her desires make it all so arousing. There'll be times when she'd prefer him to do big things, like throw her down on the bed like a damsel in distress at the hands of a wicked villain. She simply has to tell him the fantasy and he'll be happy to oblige, but that rather takes away the element of surprise! The next time he hopes to excite her with this scenario, she'll have another fantasy in mind, which all goes to show that, because he uses his head and not his heart to probe her mysterious secrets, the way to this girl's pleasure continually eludes him. Still, if he doesn't mind the chase, she certainly won't mind trying to get away.